Object-Oriented Programming

Design Principles

Design Patterns

With C#

If you have any questions, comments, or feedback about this book, I would love to hear from you.

Please feel free to reach out to me via email:

Email: ec.books.contact@gmail.com

Table of Contents

Prerequisites

C# - Preferred or at least Java, look for the book Eldar CSharp C# at amazon.

https://www.amazon.com/s?k=Eldar+CSharp+C%23

Object-Oriented Programming

Object-Oriented Programming (OOP) is a programming paradigm that is based on the concept of "objects." It is a fundamental and widely used approach in software development that helps in designing and organizing code in a more modular and maintainable way.

Class: A class is a template for creating objects. A class encapsulates both data (attributes) and the methods (functions) that operate on that data.

Object: Object is instance of class. In OOP, everything is treated as an object. Objects can interact with each other to perform various tasks.

```csharp
//objects template
public class User
{
    //3 attributes
    public string Name { get; set; }
    public string Email { get; set; }
    public string PhoneNumber { get; set; }

    //function/method
    public void PrintName()
    {
        Console.WriteLine(Name);
    }
}
```

```csharp
//instance of an object
User u1 = new() { Name = "Eldar" };

//instance of an object
User u2 = new() { Name = "David" };

//call methods
u1.PrintName();// Output: Eldar
u2.PrintName();// Output: David
```

Encapsulation

Encapsulation is one of the fundamental principles of object-oriented programming (OOP) that involves the bundling of data (attributes) and methods (functions) that operate on the data into a single unit, which is called a class.

In the example above, encapsulation is used to group related data and behavior together within the User class.

Attributes (Data Fields):

The User class has three attributes: 'Name', 'Email', and 'PhoneNumber'. These attributes store information about a user.

Method (Function):

The User contains a method called 'PrintName()'. This method is responsible for printing the user's name to the console.

Inheritance

Inheritance is a fundamental object-oriented programming (OOP) concept that allows you to create a new class (called a derived or subclass) based on an existing class (called a base or parent class), the derived class inherits the attributes and behaviors (fields, properties, methods) of the base class, which promotes code reuse and the creation of a hierarchical structure among classes.

```
public class User
{
    public string Name;
    public string Email;
    public string PhoneNumber;

}
public class AdminUser : User
{

}
```

In this example, the 'AdminUser' class is an extension of the 'User' class, and it benefits from the attributes and behaviors defined in the 'User' class, facilitating code reuse and allowing you to create specialized classes like AdminUser with a common set of properties and methods from the base class.

Polymorphism

Polymorphism is one of the fundamental concepts in object-oriented programming. It allows objects of different classes to be treated as objects of a common base class or interface, enabling code to work with objects in a more generic and flexible way.

```csharp
public class User
{
    public string Name;
    public string Email;
    public string PhoneNumber;

    public virtual string GetRole()
    {
        return "User";
    }

}

public class AdminUser : User
{
    public override string GetRole()
    {
        return "Admin";
    }
}

public class PremiumUser : User
{
    public override string GetRole()
    {
        return "PremiumUser";
    }
}
```

In this code, you can create instances of the User, 'AdminUser', and 'PremiumUser' classes. Each instance has access to the' GetRole()' method. When you call 'GetRole()' on these instances, you get the specific role associated with each class. This demonstrates the concept of method overriding, where derived classes provide their implementations of methods defined in the base class while inheriting other properties and methods from the base class.

```
List<User> list = new();
list.Add(new User());
list.Add(new AdminUser());
list.Add(new PremiumUser());

foreach (var u in list)
{
    Console.WriteLine(u.GetRole());
}
/*
Output:
User
Admin
PremiumUser
*/
```

The List<User> is a generic list that can hold objects of the 'User' class or any of its derived classes (AdminUser and PremiumUser) because of polymorphism. When you add objects of derived classes to a list of the base class, you can treat all of them as instances of the base class while still being able to access their overridden methods.

In the foreach loop, you iterate through each object in the list. Even though you are iterating through a list of User objects, the overridden GetRole() method in each derived class will be called, and the role associated with each specific object type will be displayed.

Abstraction

Abstraction is the process of simplifying complex reality by modeling classes based on their essential characteristics. It hides the complex, non-essential details and exposes only the relevant information.

Code should depend on abstractions (e.g., interfaces or abstract classes) rather than concrete implementations

```
public abstract class User
{
    public string Name;
    public string Email;
    public string PhoneNumber;
    public abstract string GetRole();

}

public class AdminUser : User
{
    public override string GetRole()
    {
        return "Admin";
    }
}

public class RegularUser : User
{
    public override string GetRole()
    {
        return "RegularUser";
    }
}
```

This code illustrates the concept of abstraction and method overriding. The abstract base class User defines a common interface for its derived classes to follow, ensuring that each derived class provides its own implementation for the 'GetRole()' method. This promotes a structured and consistent way of representing different roles for users while hiding the specific implementation details of each role within its respective class.

Design Principles

Design principles in software engineering are fundamental guidelines and best practices that help in creating software that is maintainable, scalable, and efficient. These principles serve as a foundation for designing and architecting software systems.

While software design principles are valuable and can result in more maintainable, extensible, and organized code, they are not absolute requirements for every software project. The application of these principles should be based on the specific needs and goals of the project. There's no need to feel obligated to enforce any particular principles.

Here are some key aspects of design principles in general:

Modularity: is the concept of breaking down a system into smaller, self-contained, and independent modules. Each module handles a specific aspect of the system, which enhances maintainability and reusability.

Decoupling: is about reducing interdependencies between software components. Loosely coupled systems are more adaptable, as changes in one component don't have a ripple effect throughout the entire system.

Flexibility: Design principles encourage flexibility in software systems. A well-designed system should be able to accommodate changes and new requirements with minimal impact on existing components.

Scalability: principles guide the design of systems so that they can efficiently handle increased workloads as the system grows. Horizontal and vertical scalability are key considerations.

Simplicity: in design is the idea of making software systems as simple as possible without sacrificing functionality. Simple designs are easier to understand and maintain.

Consistency: in design promotes using the same patterns, conventions, and naming throughout a system. It makes the codebase more readable and helps in maintaining a uniform style.

Testability: is the design principle that emphasizes the importance of making software components easy to test. It leads to higher code quality and faster development cycles.

Resilience: software design principles involve building systems that can recover from errors, faults, or unexpected conditions. This ensures uninterrupted operation.

Extensibility: systems can be easily enhanced or extended without significant modifications to existing code. This is important for accommodating new features and requirements.

Minimization of Dependencies: Reducing dependencies on external libraries or components can improve software stability, as fewer points of potential failure exist.

Documentation: Documentation is an essential design principle. Well-documented code and system architecture help in understanding, maintaining, and scaling the software.

Usability: Design principles also apply to user interfaces and user experience (UX). Usability principles guide the creation of interfaces that are intuitive and user-friendly.

Security: is a critical design principle, ensuring that systems are protected against threats, vulnerabilities, and unauthorized access.

SOLID

SOLID is an acronym that represents a set of five design principles in object-oriented programming, **S**RP, **O**CP, **L**SP, **I**SP, **D**IP. These principles help in creating well-structured, maintainable, and extensible software systems.

SRP - Single Responsibility Principle

OCP - Open/Closed Principle

LSP - Liskov Substitution Principle

ISP - Interface Segregation Principle

DIP - Dependency Inversion Principle

SRP - Single Responsibility Principle

This principle states that a class should have a single responsibility, meaning it should have only one job or function. If a class has multiple responsibilities, it becomes more difficult to maintain and modify.

Bad Example (SRP Violation)

In the SRP-violating example, the User class has multiple responsibilities, including validation and database operations.

```
public class User
{
    public string Name;
    public string Email;
    public string PhoneNumber;

    // Violating SRP - validation logic within User class
    public bool ValidateUser()
    {
        // Validation logic
        return true;
    }

    // Violating SRP - database operations within User class
    public void SaveUser()
    {
        // Database insertion logic
    }

    public User GetUserById(int userId)
    {
        // Database retrieval logic
        return null;
    }
}
```

Good Example (SRP-Compliant)

In the SRP-compliant example, the User class has a single, well-defined responsibility, managing user information. Any other responsibilities, such as validation or database operations, are delegated to separate classes.

```csharp
public class User
{
    public string Name;
    public string Email;
    public string PhoneNumber;
}

// Separate class for validation
public class UserValidator
{
    public bool ValidateUser(User user)
    {
        // Validation logic
        return true;
    }
}

// Separate class for database operations
public class UserRepository
{
    public void SaveUser(User user)
    {
        // Database insertion logic
    }

    public User GetUserById(int userId)
    {
        // Database retrieval logic
        return null;
    }
}
```

OCP - Open/Closed Principle

Software entities (classes, modules, functions, etc.) should be open for extension but closed for modification. This means you can add new functionality to a class without changing its existing code. You achieve this through inheritance, interfaces, and abstract classes.

Bad Example (OCP Violation)

In the OCP-violating example, we modify the existing User class to add new functionality. This violates the OCP principle because it requires changing the existing class.

```csharp
public class User
{
    public string Name;
    public string Email;
    public string PhoneNumber;
    public bool IsPremium;// New property added

    public void UpgradeAccount()
    {
        if (!IsPremium)
        {
            // Custom logic to upgrade the user to a premium account
            IsPremium = true;
        }
    }

    public void ManageUsers()
    {
        if (IsPremium)
        {
            // Custom logic to manage other users
        }
    }
}
```

In this example, we violated the OCP by modifying the existing User class to add new properties and methods. This approach can introduce complexity and may require changes throughout the codebase, potentially affecting existing functionality.

Good Example (OCP-Compliant)

13

In the OCP-compliant example, we extend the functionality of the User class by creating new classes that inherit from User. This allows us to add new features without modifying the existing User class.

```
public class User
{
    public string Name;
    public string Email;
    public string PhoneNumber;
}

public class PremiumUser : User
{
    public void UpgradeAccount()
    {
        // Custom logic to upgrade a user to a premium account
    }
}

public class AdminUser : User
{
    public void ManageUsers()
    {
        // Custom logic to manage other users(
        //e.g., create, update, delete)
    }
}
```

In this example, the User class remains closed for modification, and new features like UpgradeAccount and ManageUsers are added by creating new classes (PremiumUser and AdminUser) that inherit from User. This approach adheres to the OCP.

LSP - Liskov Substitution Principle

The principle was initially introduced by Barbara Liskov. It states that a subclass should be able to replace its base class without causing issues or breaking the program.

Bad Example (LSP Violation)

In the LSP-violating example, the 'AdminUser' class introduces a method that the base 'User' class doesn't have, and using it in place of a 'User' object could lead to issues.

```csharp
public class User
{
    public string Name;
    public string Email;
    public string PhoneNumber;
    public string Role;

}
public class AdminUser : User
{
    public string GetRole()
    {
        return Role;
    }
}
```

The issue with this code is that it violates the Liskov Substitution Principle because the 'AdminUser' class introduces a method (GetRole) that does not exist in the base class (User). In LSP-compliant code, derived classes should be substitutable for their base classes without introducing new members or behaviors that are not present in the base class.

Good Example (LSP-Compliant)

Here, you have a base class 'User' with a method 'GetRole', and a derived class AdminUser that overrides this method to provide a different implementation.

```
public class User
{
   public string Name;
   public string Email;
   public string PhoneNumber;

   public virtual string GetRole()
   {
      return "User";
   }
}
public class AdminUser : User
{
   public override string GetRole()
   {
      return "Admin";
   }
}
```

The 'AdminUser' class, which is derived from User, is a valid substitution for its base class. This is because when you call 'GetRole' on an instance of 'AdminUser', it returns "Admin," which is an extension of the behavior defined in the base class User, where 'GetRole' returns "User."

ISP - Interface Segregation Principle

Clients should not be forced to depend on interfaces they do not use. This principle suggests that you should have small, specific interfaces rather than large, monolithic ones. Clients should only be required to implement the methods that are relevant to them.

Bad Example (ISP Violation)

```csharp
public interface IUser
{
    string Name { get; set; }
    string Email { get; set; }
    void Login();
    void Logout();
}

public class User : IUser
{
    public string Name { get; set; }
    public string Email { get; set; }

    public void Login()
    {
        //logic
    }

    public void Logout()
    {
        //logic
    }
}
```

In this bad example, a single monolithic interface, IUser, is used for all aspects of user functionality. If a class, such as User, implements this interface, it is forced to provide implementations for all members of the interface, even if it doesn't use all of them.

The bad example violates the ISP because it creates a situation where clients may be required to implement methods they don't need or use, leading to unnecessary coupling and complexity.

Good Example (ISP-Compliant)

```csharp
public class User : IUserInformation, IUserActions
{
    public string Name { get; set; }
    public string Email { get; set; }
    public void Login()
    {
        //logic
    }
    public void Logout()
    {
        //logic
    }
}

public interface IUserInformation
{
    string Name { get; set; }
    string Email { get; set; }
}

public interface IUserActions
{
    void Login();
    void Logout();
}
```

Two specific interfaces, 'IUserInformation' and 'IUserActions', are created to represent different aspects of a user's functionality.

The User class implements only the interfaces that are relevant to its functionality, ensuring that clients (classes that use the User class) are not forced to depend on interfaces they don't use.

DIP - Dependency Inversion Principle

High-level modules should not depend on low-level modules. Both should depend on abstractions. Additionally, abstractions should not depend on details, details should depend on abstractions. This principle encourages the use of interfaces or abstract classes to define dependencies, allowing for greater flexibility and easier changes to implementations.

Bad Example (DIP Violation)

```
public class User
{
    public User GetUserById(int userId)
    {
        // Retrieve user from a data source
        return new User();
    }

    public void SaveUser(User user)
    {
        // Save user to a data source
    }
}
```

In this bad example, the 'User' class contains both high-level business logic and low-level data access logic. This tightly couples the high-level and low-level logic, violating the DIP.

Good Example (DIP-Compliant)

```csharp
// Define an interface for a user repository
public interface IUserRepository
{
    User GetUserById(int userId);
    void SaveUser(User user);
}

// High-level module (business logic)
// depends on the IUserRepository abstraction
public class UserManager
{
    private IUserRepository userRepository;

    public UserManager(IUserRepository userRepository)
    {
        this.userRepository = userRepository;
    }

    public User GetUser(int userId)
    {
        return userRepository.GetUserById(userId);
    }

    public void CreateUser(User user)
    {
        userRepository.SaveUser(user);
    }
}

// Low-level module (data access)
// implements the IUserRepository interface
public class UserRepository : IUserRepository
{
    public User GetUserById(int userId)
    {
        // Retrieve user from a data source
        return new User();
    }

    public void SaveUser(User user)
    {
        // Save user to a data source
    }
}
```

We have an 'IUserRepository' interface representing user data access methods.

The 'UserManager' class (high-level module) depends on the 'IUserRepository' abstraction through constructor injection.

The 'UserRepository' class (low-level module) implements the 'IUserRepository' interface.

This example adheres to the DIP by ensuring that high-level and low-level modules depend on abstractions (the IUserRepository interface), allowing for easy substitution of the data access implementation without affecting the high-level logic.

IoC - Inversion of control

Inversion of Control (IoC) is a design principle and a concept in software engineering that refers to a programming paradigm in which the control over the flow of a program's execution is shifted from the program itself to a framework or container. This paradigm is often used to achieve greater flexibility, modularity, and maintainability in software systems.

Without IoC

```csharp
public class EmailService
{
    public void Send(string message)
    {
        // send email logic
    }
}

public class SmsService
{
    public void Send(string message)
    {
        // send sms logic
    }
}

EmailService emailSvc = new();
SmsService smsSvc = new();

emailSvc.Send("Hi");
smsSvc.Send("Hi");
```

The code demonstrates two classes, 'EmailService' and 'SmsService', each with a Send method for sending email and SMS messages, respectively. You then create instances of these classes and use them to send messages.

```csharp
public interface INotificationService
{
    void Send(string message);
}

public class EmailService : INotificationService
{
    public void Send(string message)
    {
        // send email logic
    }
}

public class SmsService : INotificationService
{
    public void Send(string message)
    {
        // send sms logic
    }
}
```

```csharp
INotificationService notificationService;

var useEmailService = true;

if (useEmailService)
{
    notificationService = new EmailService();
}
else
{
    notificationService = new SmsService();
}

notificationService.Send("Hi");
```

The key IoC concept in this code is that the control over which 'INotificationService' implementation to use is external to the service itself. This allows you to change the behavior of your application by changing the implementation of the 'INotificationService' without directly modifying the client code. This decoupling between the client and the concrete implementations is one of the core principles of IoC.

DI - Dependency Injection

Dependency Injection (DI) is a design principle and technique in software development that promotes the inversion of the control of dependencies in an application. It is a crucial part of achieving Inversion of Control (IoC) and is widely used in various programming paradigms, including object-oriented programming.

While DI is often associated with IoC, it's also a standalone design principle. It promotes the injection of dependencies (e.g., services, components) into a class or module, rather than having the class create its dependencies. This enhances modularity and testability.

```
var emailService = new EmailService();
// Manually inject dependency
var notificationClient = new NotificationClient(emailService);

public class EmailService
{
    public void Send(string message)
    {
        // send email logic
    }
}

public class NotificationClient
{
    private readonly EmailService emailSvc;

    public NotificationClient(EmailService emailSvc)
    {
        this.emailSvc = emailSvc;
    }
}
```

The 'NotificationClient' class takes an 'EmailService' instance through its constructor, and you manually create instances of both the 'EmailService' and 'NotificationClient'. This approach allows you to perform Dependency Injection.

Built in DI in C# applications

```csharp
public interface INotificationService
{
    void Send(string message);
}

public class EmailService : INotificationService
{
    public void Send(string message)
    {
        // send email logic
    }
}

public class NotificationClient
{
    private readonly INotificationService notificationSvc;

    public NotificationClient(
                INotificationService notificationSvc)
    {
        this.notificationSvc = notificationSvc;
    }
    public void Send(string message)
    {
        notificationSvc.Send(message);
    }

}
```

```csharp
using Microsoft.Extensions.DependencyInjection;

var serviceProvider = new ServiceCollection()
        .AddScoped<INotificationService,EmailService>()
        .AddScoped<NotificationClient>()
        .BuildServiceProvider();

NotificationClient notificationClient =
serviceProvider.GetRequiredService<NotificationClient>();

notificationClient.Send("Hi");
```

The control over the creation and injection of dependencies is managed by the DI container. It also makes it easy to swap out different implementations of 'INotificationService' without changing the client code.

TDA - Tell, Don't Ask

A software design principle that encourages developers to encapsulate behavior within objects and to avoid excessive querying of an object's state to make decisions. Instead of asking an object about its state and then making a decision based on that state, you should tell the object what you want it to do. This approach promotes better object-oriented design, improves encapsulation, and reduces coupling between objects.

```
// Asking (not recommended)
if (car.IsOutOfFuel())
{
    car.Refuel();
}

// Telling (recommended)
car.Refuel();
```

Fail-Safe Defaults

This principle recommends setting safe default behaviors or configurations to ensure that a system remains functional or secure even if explicit configuration is missing or incorrect.

```
int GetTimeout()
{
    return 60;
}
```

```
int timeoutInSeconds = GetTimeout();

// Apply a failsafe default in case the configuration
// is missing or invalid
if (timeoutInSeconds <= 0)
{
    // Use a 30second timeout as a safe default.
    timeoutInSeconds = 30;
}
```

Separation of Immutable and Mutable States

Promotes separating data that doesn't change (immutable) from data that can change (mutable). This separation helps maintain data integrity, reduce complexity, and improve the predictability and robustness of the software.

```csharp
// Immutable data representing a point in 2D space
public record Point(int X, int Y);

// Mutable data representing a list of points
public class PointList
{
    private List<Point> points = new List<Point>();

    public void AddPoint(Point point)
    {
        points.Add(point);
    }

    public IReadOnlyList<Point> GetPoints()
    {
        return points.AsReadOnly();
    }
}
```

```csharp
PointList pointList = new PointList();
pointList.AddPoint(new Point(1, 2));
pointList.AddPoint(new Point(3, 4));

// Attempt to modify an immutable Point
// compile error:
pointList.GetPoints()[0] = new Point(5, 6);
```

The 'Point' data is immutable, and it's used to represent a point in 2D space. The 'PointList' class is responsible for managing a list of points, and it keeps the list mutable. By separating the immutable Point instances from the mutable list, we maintain data integrity and prevent accidental modification of the individual points.

Behavioral Types

Behavioral types specify expected behaviors and interactions of components in a system, enhancing the predictability and reliability of distributed systems.

```
class LightSwitch
{
    private enum State
    {
        Off,
        On,
    }

    private State currentState;

    public LightSwitch()
    {
        currentState = State.Off;
    }

    public void TurnOn()
    {
        if (currentState == State.Off)
        {
            Console.WriteLine("Turning the light on.");
            currentState = State.On;
        }
        else
        {
            Console.WriteLine("The light is already on.");
        }
    }

    public void TurnOff()
    {
        if (currentState == State.On)
        {
            Console.WriteLine("Turning the light off.");
            currentState = State.Off;
        }
        else
        {
            Console.WriteLine("The light is already off.");
        }
    }
}
```

```
LightSwitch lightSwitch = new LightSwitch();

lightSwitch.TurnOn(); // Turning the light on.
lightSwitch.TurnOn(); // The light is already on.
lightSwitch.TurnOff(); // Turning the light off.
lightSwitch.TurnOff(); // The light is already off.
```

The LightSwitch class represents a simple light switch with two states: On and Off.

The TurnOn and TurnOff methods allow you to interact with the light switch. The behavior of the light switch is specified through conditional checks in these methods.

The FSM approach is used to ensure that the light can only be turned on when it's off and vice versa. It enforces a basic behavioral constraint.

While this example simplifies the concept of behavioral types, in practice, behavioral types are often more formally defined and are frequently used in more complex scenarios, such as in distributed systems, concurrent programming, and formal verification. In those cases, more advanced tools and formal methods are employed to specify and analyze system behavior.

Self-Documenting Code

The principle of writing code in a way that is so clear and expressive that it acts as its own documentation, reducing the need for extensive comments.

```
public class Calculator
{
    // A well-named method that performs addition
    public int Add(int operand1, int operand2)
    {
        return operand1 + operand2;
    }
    // Clear code structure with consistent indentation
    public int Subtract(int operand1, int operand2)
    {
        return operand1 - operand2;
    }
}
```

SPOT - Single Point of Truth

The SPOT principle promotes the idea that there should be a single authoritative source for specific information, such as configuration values or business rules.

```csharp
public class AppConfiguration
{
    // SPOT for configuration settings
    public static string ApiBaseUrl { get; } =
                        "https://api.example.com";
    public static int MaxRetryAttempts { get; } = 3;
}

public class ApiClient
{
    public void Connect()
    {
        string apiBaseUrl = AppConfiguration.ApiBaseUrl;

        // Connect to the API using the API base URL
        Console.WriteLine($"Connected to API at {apiBaseUrl}");
    }
}
```

```csharp
ApiClient apiClient = new ApiClient();

// Access configuration settings from the SPOT
string apiBaseUrl = AppConfiguration.ApiBaseUrl;
int maxRetryAttempts = AppConfiguration.MaxRetryAttempts;
apiClient.Connect();
```

By centralizing configuration settings in a dedicated class, you adhere to the SPOT principle. If you need to update a configuration setting, you only need to do it in one place (the AppConfiguration class), and those changes are reflected consistently throughout the application. This prevents redundancy, reduces the risk of inconsistent values, and simplifies maintenance.

CoI - Composition Over Inheritance

Favors object composition (combining smaller objects) over class inheritance for code reuse. Reduces the complexity and tight coupling associated with deep inheritance hierarchies.

```csharp
class Animal
{
    public void Eat() { Console.WriteLine("Animal is eating."); }
}
// Using inheritance
class Dog : Animal
{
    public void Bark() { Console.WriteLine("Dog is barking."); }
}

// Using composition
class DogWithComposition
{
    private readonly Animal animal;

    public DogWithComposition(Animal animal)
    {
        this.animal = animal;
    }

    public void Bark() { Console.WriteLine("Dog is barking."); }

    // Delegating the Eat behavior to the composed Animal object
    public void Eat() { animal.Eat(); }
}
```

The first approach uses class inheritance to create a 'Dog' class, which inherits the 'Eat' method from the base 'Animal' class. The second approach uses composition to create a 'DogWithComposition' class that contains an instance of the 'Animal' class. The 'Bark' method is added directly to the 'DogWithComposition' class, and the 'Eat' behavior is delegated to the composed 'Animal' object.

DSL - Domain-Specific Language

A DSL is a programming language or specification language dedicated to a particular problem domain, a particular problem representation technique, and a particular problem solution technique.

```csharp
public class Business
{
    private readonly List<Func<Order, bool>> rules = new();

    public void AddRule(Func<Order, bool> rule)
    {
        rules.Add(rule);
    }

    public bool Evaluate(Order order)
    {
        return rules.All(rule => rule(order));
    }
}

public class Order
{
    public int TotalAmount { get; set; }
    public string DiscountCode { get; set; }
}

public class BusinessRules
{
    public static bool IsLargeOrder(Order order) =>
                    order.TotalAmount >= 1000;
    public static bool HasDiscountCode(Order order) =>
            !string.IsNullOrEmpty(order.DiscountCode);
}
```

```csharp
var business = new Business();
business.AddRule(BusinessRules.IsLargeOrder);
business.AddRule(BusinessRules.HasDiscountCode);

Order order1=new{ TotalAmount = 1200, DiscountCode = "SAVE5" };
Order order2=new{ TotalAmount = 800, DiscountCode = "SUMMER10" };

Console.WriteLine(business.Evaluate(order1)); // true
Console.WriteLine(business.Evaluate(order2)); // false
```

We create a simple internal DSL for defining business rules using functions and the 'BusinessRule' class. It allows the easy specification and evaluation of rules for different orders, demonstrating how an internal DSL can make expressing domain-specific rules more natural and readable.

DRY - Don't Repeat Yourself

A principle that encourages avoiding code duplication by reusing existing code or creating abstractions to eliminate redundancy.

```
public class Calculator
{
    public int Add(int a, int b) => a + b;
    public int Subtract(int a, int b) => a - b;
    public int Multiply(int a, int b) => a * b;
    public int Divide(int a, int b)
    {
        if (b == 0)
        {
            Console.WriteLine("Division by zero is not allowed.");
            return 0;
        }
        return a / b;
    }
}

Calculator calculator = new();
int result1 = calculator.Add(10, 5);
int result2 = calculator.Subtract(20, 8);
int result3 = calculator.Multiply(7, 3);
int result4 = calculator.Divide(15, 3);
```

The 'Calculator' class follows the DRY principle by defining reusable methods for arithmetic operations. The Divide method also checks for division by zero, promoting error prevention and consistency.

WET - We Enjoy Typing

WET emphasizes the importance of clarity over brevity, especially in the case of complex or tricky code. WET duplicates unnecessarily code, while "DRY" aims to reduce redundancy and make the code more maintainable and efficient.

LoD - Law of Demeter

Also known as the "Principle of Least Knowledge," it encourages objects to interact with only their immediate neighbors and avoid excessive knowledge of other objects' internal details. Promotes loose coupling and encapsulation.

```csharp
public class Team
{
    private List<Player> players = new();
    public void AddPlayer(Player player)
    {
        players.Add(player);
    }
    public void PrintPlayers()
    {
        foreach (var player in players)
        {
            Console.WriteLine(player.Name);
        }
    }
}

public class Player
{
    public string Name { get; set; }

    public Player(string name)
    {
        Name = name;
    }
}
```

```csharp
Team team = new Team();

Player player1 = new Player("Eldar");
Player player2 = new Player("David");

team.AddPlayer(player1);
team.AddPlayer(player2);
```

The 'Team' object adheres to the Law of Demeter. It does not expose the internal 'Player' objects directly. Instead, it provides a method, 'PrintPlayers()', to access and display the player names.

YAGNI - You Ain't Gonna Need It

This principle advises against adding functionality or complexity to your codebase until it's actually needed. Avoid over-engineering by focusing on the current requirements.

```csharp
// Process payment only if necessary
if (order.TotalAmount > 0)
{
    order.ProcessPayment();
}

public class Order
{
    public int OrderId;
    public string CustomerName;
    public decimal TotalAmount;

    public void ProcessPayment()
    {
        // Simulate payment processing
        Console.WriteLine($"Payment processed");
    }
}

Order order = new Order
{
    OrderId = 1,
    CustomerName = "Eldar",
    TotalAmount = 80M
};
```

The 'Order' class contains a 'ProcessPayment' method, which simulates payment processing. However, the payment is processed only if the 'TotalAmount' is greater than zero. This follows the YAGNI principle by avoiding unnecessary payment processing for orders with a zero total. It keeps the code simple and focused on the immediate need.

KISS - Keep It Simple, Stupid

Simplicity is key. Keep your code, design, and architecture as simple as possible to make it more understandable and maintainable.

```
public class Calculator
{
    public int Add(int a, int b)
    {
        return a + b;
    }

    public int Subtract(int a, int b)
    {
        return a - b;
    }
}
```

Law of Clarity

Code should be written with clarity and understandability in mind. Avoid cryptic names, complex nested structures, and excessive cleverness.

Law of Good Names

Use descriptive and meaningful names for variables, functions, classes, and other elements. A good name can make code self-explanatory.

SoC - Separation of Concerns

Divide your software into distinct modules or components, each handling a specific concern or responsibility. This enhances maintainability and testability.

```
// Data Storage Concern
public class DataStorage
{
    private List<string> data = new();

    public void StoreData(string item)
    {
        data.Add(item);
    }
```

```csharp
   public List<string> GetData()
   {
      return data;
   }

}

// Process Data Concern
public class ProcessData
{
   private List<string> data;

   public ProcessData(List<string> data)
   {
      this.data = data;
   }
   public void Print()
   {
      foreach (var item in data)
      {
         Console.WriteLine(item);
      }
   }
}

DataStorage storage = new();
storage.StoreData("Item 1");
storage.StoreData("Item 2");

ProcessData processData = new(storage.GetData());
processData.Print();
```

The 'DataStorage' class is responsible for storing data.

The 'ProcessData' class is responsible for the data logic.

Both concerns are separated into their respective classes, and the data is passed between them as needed. This separation promotes clarity and maintainability, and it allows each class to focus on its specific concern.

CQS - Command-Query Separation

A design principle that states that a method should be either a command that performs an action or a query that returns data, but not both. This enhances code clarity.

Fail Fast

Detect and handle errors or invalid inputs as early as possible in your code. Fail quickly to prevent issues from propagating.

Law of Leaky Abstractions

Acknowledges that all abstractions are leaky to some extent. It's important to understand the underlying system when working with abstractions.

This principle states that, while abstractions and higher-level frameworks are designed to simplify and hide the complexities of underlying systems, they are never perfect, and the underlying details can "leak" through.

POLS - Principle of Least Surprise

Code should behave in a way that's least surprising to the user or developer. Consistency is key.

The Law of Triviality (Bikeshedding):

Also known as Parkinson's Law of Triviality, it suggests that people tend to spend a disproportionate amount of time on trivial issues while avoiding the more complex ones. It's a reminder to focus on what truly matters in design discussions.

Cohesion and Coupling

High cohesion implies that related functionality should be in the same module or class. Low coupling means that modules or classes should have minimal dependencies on each other.

The Rule of Three

When the same code is duplicated in two places, it's a sign of coincidence. When the same code is duplicated in three places, it's time to create a shared function or module.

Duck Typing

A concept in dynamic languages where the type or class of an object is determined by its behavior (methods and properties) rather than its explicit type declaration.

```csharp
public interface ISpeak
{
    string Speak();
}

// Classes implementing the ISpeaker interface
public class Dog : ISpeak
{
    public string Speak()
    {
        return "Woof!";
    }
}

public class Duck : ISpeak
{
    public string Speak()
    {
        return "Quack!";
    }
}

public static void AnimalSpeak<T>(T animal) where T : ISpeak
{
    Console.WriteLine(animal.Speak());
}
```

```csharp
Dog dog = new();
Duck duck = new();

AnimalSpeak(dog); // Outputs: "Woof"
AnimalSpeak(duck); // Outputs: "Quack"
```

The 'ISpeak' interface defines a method 'Speak()'. The 'AnimalSpeak' method uses a generic type constraint (where T : ISpeaker) to ensure that it works with any object implementing the 'ISpeaker' interface. This approach allows for similar behavior to duck typing, as the method accepts any object that "quacks like a duck" (implements ISpeaker) without checking the specific type of the object.

BDD - Behavior-Driven Development

An approach that encourages developers to write tests that specify the expected behavior of the system from the user's perspective before implementing the code.

DDD - Domain-Driven Design

A design approach that emphasizes understanding and modeling the problem domain within the software design. It encourages close collaboration between domain experts and developers.

Feature Flag/Feature Toggle

The practice of using feature toggles or flags to enable or disable specific features at runtime. This allows for controlled rollouts and experimentation.

```
IConfigurationRoot configuration = new ConfigurationBuilder()
        .AddJsonFile("appsettings.json")
        .Build();

bool isPaymentFeatureEnabled =
            configuration.GetValue<bool>("paymentFeature");

if (isPaymentFeatureEnabled)
{
    Console.WriteLine("New feature is enabled.");
}
else
{
    Console.WriteLine("New feature is disabled.");
}
```

Feature toggles are useful for making changes to your application without deploying new code, enabling you to control features in production without the need for immediate code changes. This can be valuable for managing feature releases, conducting experiments, and ensuring a smooth user experience.

Time-Tested Principle

New code should be written in a way that makes it easier to test and verify its correctness.

Design patterns

Design patterns are recurring solutions to common problems in software design. They provide a structured and time-tested way to solve design problems and create more maintainable and flexible software. Design patterns are not complete designs or libraries but templates that can be applied to various situations.

Creational Patterns

Creational design patterns deal with the process of object creation, trying to make it more flexible and efficient. They provide ways to create objects while hiding the creation logic, rather than instantiating objects directly using constructors.

Lazy Initialization Pattern

Delays the creation or initialization of an object until it is first accessed.

Useful when you want to minimize the cost of initializing an object that might not be needed.

```csharp
public class ExpensiveResource
{
    public ExpensiveResource()
    {
        Console.WriteLine("Creating an expensive resource.");
    }

    public void UseResource()
    {
        Console.WriteLine("Using the expensive resource.");
    }
}

public class LazyInitializer<T>
{
    private T instance;
    private readonly Func<T> factory;
    private bool isInitialized = false;

    public LazyInitializer(Func<T> factory)
    {
        this.factory = factory ??
            throw new ArgumentNullException(nameof(factory));
    }

    public T Value
    {
        get
        {
            if (!isInitialized)
            {
                instance = factory();
                isInitialized = true;
            }
            return instance;
        }
    }
}
```

```csharp
var lazyResource = new LazyInitializer<ExpensiveResource>(() => new());
```

```
// The expensive resource is not created until first access
Console.WriteLine("Accessing the expensive resource for the first time...");
lazyResource.Value.UseResource();

// Subsequent access uses the cached resource
lazyResource.Value.UseResource();
```

We create a LazyInitializer<T> class that accepts a factory delegate to create the object.

The Value property is used to access the object, and it initializes the object by calling the factory method if it hasn't been initialized yet.

The isInitialized flag is used to track whether the object has been created.

This custom LazyInitializer<T> class provides a way to achieve lazy initialization without using the Lazy<T> class. It defers the creation of the object until the first access and then caches it for subsequent access.

Singleton Pattern

Ensures that a class has only one instance and provides a global point of access to that instance. Useful when you want to limit the number of instances of a class to just one.

```
public class Singleton
{
    // Private static instance of the Singleton class
    private static Singleton instance;

    // Private constructor to prevent the creation of multiple
    // instances
    private Singleton(){}

    // Public method to provide access to the Singleton instance
    public static Singleton GetInstance()
    {
        // If the instance does not exist, create it
        if (instance == null)
        {
            instance = new Singleton();
        }

        return instance;
    }
}
```

We have a private static field instance that holds the single instance of the Singleton class.

The constructor is made private to prevent external instantiation of the class.

We provide a public static method 'GetInstance' that returns the single instance of the Singleton class. If the instance doesn't exist, it's created before returning.

This basic Singleton pattern implementation is not thread-safe, which means it may not work correctly in a multi-threaded environment. To make it thread-safe, you can use a lock or use Lazy initialization.

With lock

```
public class Singleton
{
    private static Singleton instance;
    private static readonly object lockObject = new object();

    private Singleton(){}

    public static Singleton GetInstance()
    {
        if (instance == null)
        {
            lock (lockObject)
            {
            // Check again inside the lock to avoid race conditions
                if (instance == null)
                {
                    instance = new Singleton();
                }
            }
        }
        return instance;
    }
}
```

We use a 'lockObject' to serve as a synchronization lock for controlling access to the instance.

In the 'GetInstance' method, we first check if instance is null without acquiring the lock to improve performance. If instance is already initialized, this avoids the overhead of acquiring and releasing the lock.

If instance is null, we use a lock statement to ensure that only one thread can create the instance. We check for null again inside the lock to prevent multiple threads from initializing the instance.

Once the instance is created, subsequent calls to 'GetInstance' will return the already initialized instance without entering the lock section.

```
public class Singleton
{
    private static readonly Lazy<Singleton> lazyInstance =
            new Lazy<Singleton>(() => new Singleton());

    private Singleton() { }

    public static Singleton GetInstance()
    {
        return lazyInstance.Value;
    }
}
```

The 'lazyInstance' is thread-safe due to the nature of the Lazy<T> class in C#. The Lazy<T> class is specifically designed to ensure thread safety when initializing a value, which makes it suitable for implementing the Singleton pattern in a thread-safe manner.

Simple Factory Pattern

A factory class with a method for creating objects without exposing the creation logic. Provides a simple way to create objects without the need for explicit constructors.

Here's how the Simple Factory Pattern works:

Factory: The Factory class or method is responsible for creating objects. It provides a method or a set of methods to create objects based on the input provided.

Products: These are the objects that the factory creates. Products often share a common interface or base class. The Factory method returns an instance of one of these products.

Client: The Client is the code that uses the Factory to create objects. The Client requests objects from the Factory, and the Factory returns the appropriate product.

```csharp
// Abstract Product
public abstract class Product
{
    public abstract void Display();
}

// Concrete Products
public class ConcreteProductA : Product
{
    public override void Display()
    {
        Console.WriteLine("This is Concrete Product A.");
    }
}

public class ConcreteProductB : Product
{
    public override void Display()
    {
        Console.WriteLine("This is Concrete Product B.");
    }
}

// Factory
public class SimpleFactory
{
    public Product CreateProduct(string productType)
    {
        Product product;

        if (productType == "A")
        {
            product = new ConcreteProductA();
        }
        else if (productType == "B")
        {
            product = new ConcreteProductB();
        }
        else
        {
            throw new ArgumentException("Invalid product type");
        }

        return product;
    }
}
```

```
SimpleFactory factory = new SimpleFactory();

Product productA = factory.CreateProduct("A");
productA.Display();

Product productB = factory.CreateProduct("B");
productB.Display();
```

We have an abstract Product class that defines a common interface for products.

ConcreteProductA and ConcreteProductB are concrete implementations of the Product interface, representing different products.

SimpleFactory is responsible for creating products based on the product type specified.

In the Main method, we use the factory to create products and call the Display method on each product.

Factory Method Pattern

The Factory Method Pattern is a creational design pattern that provides an interface for creating objects but allows subclasses to alter the type of objects that will be created. This pattern promotes loose coupling between the creator (the factory) and the products it creates. It's useful when you want to decouple the client code from the specific classes it instantiates, and when you need to extend or customize object creation.

Here's how the Factory Method Pattern works:

Creator: This is an abstract class or interface that declares the factory method, which is responsible for creating products. The creator may also include some default implementation.

Concrete Creator: Subclasses of the creator provide implementations for the factory method. Each concrete creator creates a specific type of product.

Product: This is the abstract class or interface that represents the objects being created by the factory method.

Concrete Product: Subclasses of the product represent specific product types that the factory method creates.

```csharp
// Abstract Product
public abstract class Product
{
    public abstract string Description { get; }
}

// Concrete Products
public class ConcreteProduct : Product
{
    public override string Description => "Product";
}

// Abstract Creator
public abstract class Creator
{
    public abstract Product FactoryMethod();
}

// Concrete Creators
public class ConcreteCreator : Creator
{
    public override Product FactoryMethod()
    {
        return new ConcreteProduct();
    }
}
```

'Product' is an abstract class that defines the interface for products.

'ConcreteProduct' is concrete 'product' class that implement the product interface.

'Creator' is an abstract class that declares the factory method, which returns a 'Product' object.

'ConcreteCreator' and is concrete creator class that implement the factory method to create specific product.

Now, you can use the Factory Method Pattern like this:

```csharp
Creator creator = new ConcreteCreator();
Product product = creator.FactoryMethod();
Console.WriteLine(product.Description); // Output: Product
```

The Factory Method Pattern allows you to create new product types without modifying existing client code. It's a way to achieve extensibility and flexibility in your code, especially when you anticipate different variations or types of products that need to be created.

Abstract Factory Pattern

Provides an interface for creating families of related or dependent objects without specifying their concrete classes. Often used in scenarios where a system is expected to be independent of how its objects are created, composed, and represented.

Key components of the Abstract Factory Pattern include:

Abstract Factory: This is an interface or an abstract class that defines a set of factory methods for creating a family of related objects. Each factory method typically corresponds to creating an object within a particular family.

Concrete Factory: Subclasses or implementations of the abstract factory. Each concrete factory is responsible for creating the specific objects within the family. In other words, it implements the factory methods defined in the abstract factory.

Abstract Product: This is an interface or an abstract class that defines a common interface for the products created by the factory. Each product family typically has its own abstract product.

Concrete Product: Subclasses or implementations of the abstract product. Each concrete product is a specific object created by a concrete factory.

```csharp
// Abstract Product A
public abstract class AbstractProductA
{
    public abstract string GetName();
}

// Concrete Product A1
public class ConcreteProductA1 : AbstractProductA
{
    public override string GetName()
    {
        return "Product A1";
    }
}

// Abstract Factory
public interface IAbstractFactory
{
    AbstractProductA CreateProductA();
}

// Concrete Factory
public class ConcreteFactory : IAbstractFactory
{
    public AbstractProductA CreateProductA()
    {
        return new ConcreteProductA1();
    }
}
```

'IAbstractFactory' is the abstract factory interface defining factory methods for creating products.

'ConcreteFactory1' is concrete factory implementing the abstract factory interface. He creates products that belong to a specific family.

'AbstractProductA' is abstract 'product' class with a common interface.

'ConcreteProductA1' is concrete 'product' class created by the concrete factory.

You can create different families of products using the abstract factory:

```csharp
IAbstractFactory factory1 = new ConcreteFactory();
AbstractProductA productA = factory1.CreateProductA();
Console.WriteLine(productA.GetName()); // Output: Product A1
```

Builder Pattern

Separates the construction of a complex object from its representation, allowing the same construction process to create different representations. Useful when an object has a large number of parameters or complex initialization steps.

The key components of the Builder Pattern include:

Director: This is responsible for orchestrating the construction process. It interacts with the builder to build the complex object. However, the director does not need to know the specifics of how the object is constructed; it only uses the builder's interface.

Builder: This is an interface or abstract class that defines the methods for constructing the parts of the complex object. Concrete builders implement these methods to create the individual components and assemble them into the final object.

Concrete Builder: These are classes that implement the builder interface, providing specific implementations for building the complex object. A concrete builder is responsible for creating and assembling the parts of the object.

Product: This represents the complex object that you want to build. It has a structure that is defined by the builder and a set of components that make up the object.

```
// Product
public class Meal
{
    public string MainCourse { get; set; }
    public string Side { get; set; }
    public string Drink { get; set; }
    public string Dessert { get; set; }

    public override string ToString()
    {
        return $"Main Course: {MainCourse}, Side: {Side},
        Drink: {Drink}, Dessert: {Dessert}";
    }
}
```

```csharp
// Builder
public interface IMealBuilder
{
    void SetMainCourse(string mainCourse);
    void SetSide(string side);
    void SetDrink(string drink);
    void SetDessert(string dessert);
    Meal Build();
}

// Concrete Builder
public class MealBuilder : IMealBuilder
{
    private Meal meal = new Meal();

    public void SetMainCourse(string mainCourse)
    {
        meal.MainCourse = mainCourse;
    }

    public void SetSide(string side)
    {
        meal.Side = side;
    }

    public void SetDrink(string drink)
    {
        meal.Drink = drink;
    }

    public void SetDessert(string dessert)
    {
        meal.Dessert = dessert;
    }

    public Meal Build()
    {
        return meal;
    }
}
```

```csharp
// Director
public class Waiter
{
    private IMealBuilder mealBuilder;

    public Waiter(IMealBuilder builder)
    {
        mealBuilder = builder;
    }

    public void ConstructMeal()
    {
        mealBuilder.SetMainCourse("Burger");
        mealBuilder.SetSide("Fries");
        mealBuilder.SetDrink("Coke");
        mealBuilder.SetDessert("Ice Cream");
    }
}
```

```csharp
IMealBuilder builder = new MealBuilder();
Waiter waiter = new(builder);

waiter.ConstructMeal();
Meal meal = builder.Build();

Console.WriteLine(meal);
```

'Meal' is the product we want to create, with various components like main course, side, drink, and dessert.

'IMealBuilder' is the builder interface with methods for setting each part of the meal.

'MealBuilder' is a concrete builder class that implements the builder interface to create a 'Meal' object.

'Waiter' is the director that orchestrates the construction process using a specific builder.

The Builder Pattern allows you to create 'Meal' objects with different configurations by using different builders or by customizing the construction process through the builder's methods.

Prototype Pattern

Creates new objects by copying an existing object, known as the prototype.

Used when the cost of creating an object is more expensive than copying an existing one.

Key components of the Prototype Pattern include:

Prototype: This is an interface or an abstract class that defines a method for cloning itself. The concrete classes that implement this interface or extend this abstract class are considered prototypes.

Concrete Prototype: These are the concrete classes that implement the clone method defined in the prototype. They are the objects that can be cloned.

Client: The client is responsible for creating new objects by cloning the prototype. It typically uses the clone method provided by the prototype.

```
// Prototype (abstract class)
public abstract class Shape
{
    public int X { get; set; }
    public int Y { get; set; }
    public abstract Shape Clone();
    public abstract void Draw();
}

// Concrete Prototypes
public class Circle : Shape
{
    public int Radius { get; set; }

    public override Shape Clone()
    {
        return new Circle { X = this.X, Y = this.Y,
                        Radius = this.Radius };
    }

    public override void Draw()
    {
        Console.WriteLine($"Drawing a circle at ({X}, {Y})
                        with radius {Radius}");
    }
}
public class Rectangle : Shape
```

```
{
    public int Width { get; set; }
    public int Height { get; set; }

    public override Shape Clone()
    {
        return new Rectangle { X = this.X, Y = this.Y,
                Width = this.Width, Height = this.Height };
    }

    public override void Draw()
    {
        Console.WriteLine($"Drawing a rectangle at ({X}, {Y})
                with width {Width} and height {Height}");
    }
}

// Client
public class Client
{
    public Shape CreateShape(Shape prototype)
    {
        return prototype.Clone();
    }
}
```

```
var client = new Client();
var circlePrototype = new Circle { X = 10, Y = 20, Radius = 5 };
var rectanglePrototype = new Rectangle { X = 30, Y = 40, Width = 10, Height = 15 };

Shape shape1 = client.CreateShape(circlePrototype);
Shape shape2 = client.CreateShape(rectanglePrototype);

shape1.Draw();
shape2.Draw();
```

'Shape' is an abstract class representing the prototype. It defines a 'Clone' method for creating copies of shapes and a Draw method for drawing them.

'Circle' and 'Rectangle' are concrete prototypes that extend the 'Shape' class. They implement the 'Clone' method to create new instances of their respective shapes.

The 'Client' class creates new shapes by using the 'CreateShape' method, which clones the provided prototypes.

We create instances of the 'Circle' and 'Rectangle' prototypes and then use the 'Client' to create new shapes based on these prototypes.

57

The Prototype Pattern allows you to create objects with the same properties and behaviors as existing objects without having to recreate them from scratch. It's particularly useful when the process of creating an object is complex or when you want to minimize the number of subclasses for different variations of objects.

Object Pool Pattern

Manages a pool of reusable objects that can be checked out and returned when no longer needed. Improves performance by reusing objects instead of creating new ones.

Key components of the Object Pool Pattern include:

Object Pool: This is the core component that manages a collection of reusable objects. It controls object creation, allocation, and deallocation.

Client: The client is responsible for requesting objects from the object pool and returning them when no longer needed. Clients do not need to be aware of the object's creation or destruction.

Reusable Objects: These are the objects that are managed by the object pool. These objects should be designed to be reset to their initial state when returned to the pool.

```
public class ObjectPool<T>
{
    private List<T> objects = new List<T>();
    private Func<T> objectFactory;

    public ObjectPool(Func<T> objectFactory, int initialPoolSize)
    {
        this.objectFactory = objectFactory;
        for (int i = 0; i < initialPoolSize; i++)
        {
            objects.Add(objectFactory());
        }
    }


    public T BorrowObject()
    {
        if (objects.Count == 0)
```

```csharp
        {
            Console.WriteLine("No objects available.
                            Creating a new one.");
            return objectFactory();
        }

        T obj = objects[0];
        objects.RemoveAt(0);
        return obj;
    }

    public void ReturnObject(T obj)
    {
        objects.Add(obj);
    }
}

// Example usage
public class Resource
{
    public int Id { get; set; }
}
```

```csharp
// Create an object pool of Resource objects
 ObjectPool<Resource> resourcePool = new ObjectPool<Resource>(()
=> new Resource(), 3);

 // Borrow and return objects from the pool
 Resource resource1 = resourcePool.BorrowObject();
 resource1.Id = 1;
 resourcePool.ReturnObject(resource1);
 Resource resource2 = resourcePool.BorrowObject();
 resource2.Id = 2;
 Resource resource3 = resourcePool.BorrowObject();
 resource3.Id = 3;
 // Create a new object since the pool is empty
 Resource resource4 = resourcePool.BorrowObject();
 resource4.Id = 4;

 Console.WriteLine($"Resource 1 Id: {resource1.Id}");
 Console.WriteLine($"Resource 2 Id: {resource2.Id}");
 Console.WriteLine($"Resource 3 Id: {resource3.Id}");
 Console.WriteLine($"Resource 4 Id: {resource4.Id}");
```

'ObjectPool' is a generic class that manages a pool of objects. It allows objects to be borrowed and returned to the pool.

The 'Resource' class represents objects that are being managed in the object pool.

We create an object pool for Resource objects and borrow/return resources from the pool. If the pool is empty, a new object is created.

Multiton Pattern

Extends the Singleton pattern by having multiple named instances of a class, each accessible through a specific key. Useful when you want to have a single instance for each distinct key or name.

Key components of the Multiton Pattern include:

Multiton: This is the class that manages a collection of unique instances. Each instance is associated with a unique key, and the Multiton class ensures that no more than one instance exists for each key.

Instance Creation: Instances are created on demand and cached within the Multiton. When a new instance is requested with a specific key, the Multiton checks if an instance already exists for that key and returns the existing instance if found.

```csharp
// Multiton
public class Multiton
{
    private static Dictionary<string, Multiton>instances = new();
    private string key;

    private Multiton(string key)
    {
        this.key = key;
    }

    public static Multiton GetInstance(string key)
    {
        if (!instances.ContainsKey(key))
        {
            instances[key] = new Multiton(key);
        }
        return instances[key];
    }
}
```

```
   public void Display()
   {
      Console.WriteLine($"Instance with key '{key}'");
   }
}
```

The Multiton class uses a Dictionary to maintain instances associated with unique keys.

The GetInstance method is used to request a Multiton instance. It checks if an instance with the specified key exists and creates one if not.

Multiple instances can exist, each associated with a unique key.

The Display method is used to demonstrate that each instance is associated with its unique key.

Structural Patterns

Structural design patterns deal with the composition of classes or objects to form larger structures. They help in building relationships between objects and managing object hierarchies to create more efficient, flexible, and maintainable software.

Data Transfer Object

A Data Transfer Object (DTO) is a design pattern used to transfer data between software application subsystems, layers, or components. The primary purpose of a DTO is to encapsulate data and transfer it between different parts of a system in a structured and efficient manner. This pattern helps improve the separation of concerns and can enhance the maintainability and scalability of a software application.

simple example of a Data Transfer Object (DTO) in C#:

```csharp
class UserDTO
{
    public string UserId { get; set; }
    public string Name { get; set; }
    public string Email { get; set; }
}
```

The UserDTO class has properties (UserId, Name and Email) to represent the data you want to transfer.

In many cases, a simple class is used as DTO to facilitate the transfer of data between different parts of a software system. While the specific choice between using a regular class, a record, or another type may depend on the programming language and the specific requirements of the application, using a class for DTOs is a common and valid approach.

Flexibility: Classes provide a high degree of flexibility. You can define properties, methods, and additional behavior as needed. This flexibility can be beneficial if the DTO needs to encapsulate more than just simple data.

Encapsulation: Classes support encapsulation, allowing you to hide the internal details of the data structure and expose only the necessary properties and methods. This can contribute to better design and separation of concerns.

Adapter Pattern

Allows the interface of an existing class to be used as another interface. Useful when you need to adapt an existing class to work with a new interface without modifying its source code. Key components of the Adapter Pattern include:

Target: This is the interface that the client code expects to work with. It defines the operations that the client code can use.

Adaptee: This is the class or component with the incompatible interface that the client code cannot directly use.

Adapter: This is a class that bridges the gap between the Target and the Adaptee. It implements the Target interface and uses the Adaptee to perform the operations required by the Target.

```csharp
// Target interface
public interface ITarget
{
    void Request();
}

// Adaptee (incompatible interface)
public class Adaptee
{
    public void SpecificRequest()
    {
        Console.WriteLine("Adaptee's specific request.");
    }
}

// Adapter
public class Adapter : ITarget
{
    private readonly Adaptee adaptee;

    public Adapter(Adaptee adaptee)
    {
        this.adaptee = adaptee;
    }

    public void Request()
    {
        Console.WriteLine("Adapter: Translating request
                    to Adaptee's specific request.");
        adaptee.SpecificRequest();
    }
}
```

```csharp
Adaptee adaptee = new Adaptee();
ITarget adapter = new Adapter(adaptee);

adapter.Request(); // Output: Adapter: Translating request to
                    Adaptee's specific request.
```

The ITarget interface represents the interface expected by the client code, defining the Request method.

The Adaptee class has a method named SpecificRequest, which represents an incompatible interface.

63

The Adapter class implements the ITarget interface and uses an instance of the Adaptee class to perform the requested operation. It bridges the gap between the ITarget interface and the Adaptee.

We create an Adaptee instance and then use the Adapter to make the SpecificRequest method compatible with the Request method expected by the client.

The Adapter Pattern is particularly useful when integrating new code with legacy systems, working with third-party libraries, or dealing with components that have evolved over time and need to be made compatible with newer code. It allows you to encapsulate the complexity of adapting the interfaces, making the integration smoother and more maintainable.

Decorator Pattern

Attaches additional responsibilities to an object dynamically. Allows behavior to be added to individual objects without affecting the behavior of other objects from the same class.

Key components of the Decorator Pattern include:

Component: This is the abstract class or interface that defines the common interface for all concrete components and decorators.

Concrete Component: These are the concrete classes that implement the Component interface. They are the base classes to which decorators can be added.

Decorator: This is an abstract class or interface that also implements the Component interface. It contains a reference to a Component and adds additional behavior to it.

Concrete Decorator: These are concrete classes that extend the behavior of the Component and implement the Decorator interface. They wrap a Concrete Component and add functionality by delegating some or all of the operations to the Component.

```csharp
// Component
public interface Coffee
{
    string GetDescription();
    double GetCost();
}

// Concrete Component
public class SimpleCoffee : Coffee
{
    public string GetDescription()
    {
        return "Simple Coffee";
    }

    public double GetCost()
    {
        return 1.0;
    }
}

// Decorator
public abstract class CoffeeDecorator : Coffee
{
    protected Coffee decoratedCoffee;

    public CoffeeDecorator(Coffee coffee)
    {
        decoratedCoffee = coffee;
    }

    public virtual string GetDescription()
    {
        return decoratedCoffee.GetDescription();
    }

    public virtual double GetCost()
    {
        return decoratedCoffee.GetCost();
    }
}
```

```csharp
// Concrete Decorators
public class MilkDecorator : CoffeeDecorator
{
    public MilkDecorator(Coffee coffee) : base(coffee)
    {
    }

    public override string GetDescription()
    {
        return base.GetDescription() + ", with Milk";
    }

    public override double GetCost()
    {
        return base.GetCost() + 0.5;
    }
}

public class SugarDecorator : CoffeeDecorator
{
    public SugarDecorator(Coffee coffee) : base(coffee)
    {
    }

    public override string GetDescription()
    {
        return base.GetDescription() + ", with Sugar";
    }

    public override double GetCost()
    {
        return base.GetCost() + 0.2;
    }
}
```

```csharp
Coffee coffee = new SimpleCoffee();
Console.WriteLine($"Description: {coffee.GetDescription()}");
Console.WriteLine($"Cost: ${coffee.GetCost()}");

Coffee milkCoffee = new MilkDecorator(coffee);
Console.WriteLine($"Description: {milkCoffee.GetDescription()}");
Console.WriteLine($"Cost: ${milkCoffee.GetCost()}");

Coffee sweetMilkCoffee = new SugarDecorator(milkCoffee);
Console.WriteLine($"Description: {sweetMilkCoffee.GetDescription()}");
Console.WriteLine($"Cost: ${sweetMilkCoffee.GetCost()}");


/*Output:
```

Coffee is the Component interface that defines methods for getting the description and cost of a coffee.

SimpleCoffee is a Concrete Component that implements the Coffee interface.

CoffeeDecorator is the Decorator abstract class that also implements the Coffee interface. It contains a reference to a Coffee object and delegates operations to it.

MilkDecorator and SugarDecorator are Concrete Decorators that add functionality to the base coffee by extending the behavior and updating the description and cost.

We create a simple coffee, decorate it with milk, and then decorate it with sugar, each time modifying the description and cost.

Composite Pattern

Composes objects into tree structures to represent part-whole hierarchies. Allows clients to treat individual objects and compositions of objects uniformly.

Key components of the Composite Pattern include:

Component: This is the abstract class or interface that defines the common interface for all concrete objects, whether they are leaf nodes (individual objects) or composite nodes (collections of objects).

Leaf: These are the individual objects that implement the Component interface. They are the basic building blocks of the composition.

Composite: These are the objects that also implement the Component interface but can contain other components. Composites have a collection of child components and delegate operations to their children.

```csharp
// Component
public abstract class Component
{
    public string Name { get; set; }

    public Component(string name)
    {
        Name = name;
    }

    public abstract void Display(int depth);
}
// Leaf
public class Leaf : Component
{
    public Leaf(string name) : base(name) { }

    public override void Display(int depth)
    {
        Console.WriteLine(new string('-', depth) + Name);
    }
}
// Composite
public class Composite : Component
{
    private List<Component> children = new List<Component>();

    public Composite(string name) : base(name) { }

    public void Add(Component component)
    {
        children.Add(component);
    }

    public void Remove(Component component)
    {
        children.Remove(component);
    }

    public override void Display(int depth)
    {
        Console.WriteLine(new string('-', depth) + Name);
        foreach (var child in children)
        {
            child.Display(depth + 2);
        }
    }
}
Composite root = new Composite("Root");
```

68

```
root.Add(new Leaf("Leaf 1"));
root.Add(new Leaf("Leaf 2"));

Composite composite = new Composite("Composite 1");
composite.Add(new Leaf("Leaf 3"));
composite.Add(new Leaf("Leaf 4"));

root.Add(composite);

root.Display(0);

/*Output:
Root
--Leaf 1
--Leaf 2
--Composite 1
----Leaf 3
----Leaf 4
 */
```

The Component abstract class defines the common interface for both leaf nodes (e.g., Leaf) and composite nodes (e.g., Composite).

Leaf represents individual objects or leaf nodes, and Composite represents composite objects that can contain other components, including both leaf nodes and other composites.

The Display method is used to display the hierarchy of components, with the depth parameter determining the level of indentation in the output.

We create a hierarchy of components, including leaf nodes and composite nodes, and then display the entire hierarchy.

Proxy Pattern

Provides a surrogate or placeholder for another object to control access to it. Can be used for various purposes such as lazy loading, access control, monitoring, or logging.

Key components of the Proxy Pattern include:

Subject: This is the interface or abstract class that both the Real Subject and Proxy implement. It defines the common interface that the client uses to interact with the Real Subject.

Real Subject: This is the actual object with the functionality that the Proxy represents. The Real Subject implements the Subject interface.

Proxy: This is the class that acts as a surrogate for the Real Subject. The Proxy also implements the Subject interface and controls access to the Real Subject. It may add additional functionality or provide some level of control.

```csharp
// Subject
public interface IImage
{
    void Display();
}

// Real Subject
public class RealImage : IImage
{
    private string filename;

    public RealImage(string filename)
    {
        this.filename = filename;
        LoadFromDisk();
    }

    public void Display()
    {
        Console.WriteLine("Displaying " + filename);
    }

    private void LoadFromDisk()
    {
        Console.WriteLine("Loading " + filename);
    }
}
```

```
}

// Proxy
public class ImageProxy : IImage
{
   private RealImage realImage;
   private string filename;

   public ImageProxy(string filename)
   {
      this.filename = filename;
   }

   public void Display()
   {
      if (realImage == null)
      {
         realImage = new RealImage(filename);
      }
      realImage.Display();
   }
}
```

```
// Use the Proxy to control access to the Real Subject
IImage image = new ImageProxy("image.jpg");

// Display the image
image.Display();

// The Real Subject is loaded and displayed only when needed
```

The IImage interface is the Subject that defines the common interface for both RealImage and ImageProxy.

RealImage is the Real Subject that represents the actual image. It loads the image from disk and displays it.

ImageProxy is the Proxy that controls access to the Real Subject. It delays the creation and loading of the Real Image until it is actually needed.

We create an ImageProxy object to access the image. The image is loaded and displayed only when the Display method is called on the proxy.

Bridge Pattern

Separates an object's abstraction from its implementation, allowing them to vary independently. Useful when you want to avoid a permanent binding between an abstraction and its implementation.

Key components of the Bridge Pattern include:

Abstraction: This is the interface or abstract class that defines the high-level functionality that clients can use. It typically contains a reference to the Implementor.

Refined Abstraction: This is a subclass of the Abstraction that can add additional features on top of the basic functionality provided by the Abstraction.

Implementor: This is the interface or abstract class that defines the low-level operations, which are typically common to all Concrete Implementors.

Concrete Implementor: These are the classes that implement the Implementor interface. They provide the actual implementation of the low-level operations.

```csharp
// Implementor
public interface IMessageSender
{
    void SendMessage(string message);
}

// Concrete Implementors
public class EmailSender : IMessageSender
{
    public void SendMessage(string message)
    {
        Console.WriteLine("Sending email: " + message);
    }
}

public class SmsSender : IMessageSender
{
    public void SendMessage(string message)
    {
        Console.WriteLine("Sending SMS: " + message);
    }
}
```

```csharp
// Abstraction
public abstract class Message
{
    protected IMessageSender messageSender;

    public Message(IMessageSender sender)
    {
        messageSender = sender;
    }

    public abstract void Send();
}

// Refined Abstractions
public class ShortMessage : Message
{
    public ShortMessage(IMessageSender sender) : base(sender) { }

    public override void Send()
    {
        Console.WriteLine("Short message:");
        messageSender.SendMessage("This is a short message");
    }
}

public class LongMessage : Message
{
    public LongMessage(IMessageSender sender) : base(sender) { }

    public override void Send()
    {
        Console.WriteLine("Long message:");
        messageSender.SendMessage("This is a long message");
    }
}
```

```csharp
IMessageSender emailSender = new EmailSender();
IMessageSender smsSender = new SmsSender();

Message shortEmail = new ShortMessage(emailSender);
Message longSms = new LongMessage(smsSender);

shortEmail.Send();
longSms.Send();
```

73

The IMessageSender interface is the Implementor that defines the SendMessage method for sending messages.

EmailSender and SmsSender are Concrete Implementors that implement the SendMessage method for email and SMS, respectively.

The Message class is the Abstraction that holds a reference to an IMessageSender and defines the high-level method Send.

ShortMessage and LongMessage are Refined Abstractions that extend the Message class to handle different types of messages.

We create instances of EmailSender and SmsSender and use them to create ShortMessage and LongMessage instances, demonstrating how the Bridge Pattern allows different senders to work with different types of messages.

Flyweight Pattern

Minimizes memory usage or computational expenses by sharing as much as possible with related objects. Useful when you need to support a large number of objects with low overhead.

Key components of the Flyweight Pattern include:

Flyweight Interface: This is an interface or abstract class that declares the methods for the intrinsic (shared) state of the objects. The intrinsic state is the part that can be shared among multiple objects.

Concrete Flyweight: These are concrete implementations of the Flyweight interface. They store the intrinsic state and provide an implementation for any common behavior.

Flyweight Factory: This is responsible for managing and creating Flyweight objects. It typically maintains a pool of shared Flyweight objects and returns existing objects if they match the requested criteria.

Client: This is the class that uses the Flyweight objects. The Client usually stores the extrinsic (unique) state of the objects. Extrinsic state is not shared and can vary between objects.

```csharp
// Flyweight interface
public interface IShape
{
    void Draw(int x, int y);
}

// Concrete Flyweight
public class Circle : IShape
{
  private string color;

  public Circle(string color)
  {
     this.color = color;
  }

  public void Draw(int x, int y)
  {
   Console.WriteLine($"Drawing a {color} circle at ({x}, {y}).");
  }
}

// Flyweight Factory
public class ShapeFactory
{
    private Dictionary<string, IShape> shapes = new();

    public IShape GetCircle(string color)
    {
      if (!shapes.ContainsKey(color))
      {
        shapes[color] = new Circle(color);
      }
      return shapes[color];
    }
}
```

```csharp
ShapeFactory shapeFactory = new ShapeFactory();

// Client code
IShape redCircle = shapeFactory.GetCircle("Red");
IShape greenCircle = shapeFactory.GetCircle("Green");

redCircle.Draw(100, 100); //Drawing a Red circle at (100, 100)
greenCircle.Draw(200, 200);//Drawing a Green circle at (200, 200)
```

75

The IShape interface is the Flyweight interface, which defines the Draw method.

Circle is the Concrete Flyweight that stores the intrinsic state (color) and implements the Draw method.

The ShapeFactory is the Flyweight Factory, which manages the creation of Flyweight objects and shares them based on the intrinsic state (color).

The client code requests Flyweight objects (circles) from the factory and provides the extrinsic state (position) when drawing them.

Facade Pattern

Provides a simplified, unified interface to a set of interfaces in a subsystem. Helps to make a complex system easier to use by providing a high-level interface.

Key components and concepts of the Facade Pattern include:

Facade: This is the central class that acts as a simplified interface to the underlying subsystems. It encapsulates the complexity of the subsystems and provides a single, unified entry point for clients.

Subsystems: These are individual classes or components that make up the complex functionality of the system. Subsystems can be interrelated and contain their own methods and logic.

Client: The client is the class or component that interacts with the Facade to access the subsystems. The client relies on the Facade to perform various tasks without needing to interact directly with the subsystems.

```csharp
// Subsystem 1
public class CPU
{
    public void Freeze()
    {
        Console.WriteLine("CPU: Freezing...");
    }
    public void Jump(long position)
    {
        Console.WriteLine($"CPU: Jumping to memory address
                            {position}");
    }
}
```

```csharp
    public void Execute()
    {
        Console.WriteLine("CPU: Executing...");
    }
}

// Subsystem 2
public class Memory
{
    public void Load(long position, string data)
    {
        Console.WriteLine($"Memory: Loading data '{data}' to
                        memory address {position}");
    }
}

// Subsystem 3
public class HardDrive
{
    public string Read(long lba, int size)
    {
        Console.WriteLine($"Hard Drive: Reading {size} bytes from
                            LBA {lba}");
        return "Data from Hard Drive";
    }
}
// Facade
public class ComputerFacade
{
    private CPU cpu;
    private Memory memory;
    private HardDrive hardDrive;

    public ComputerFacade()
    {
        cpu = new CPU();
        memory = new Memory();
        hardDrive = new HardDrive();
    }

    public void Start()
    {
        Console.WriteLine("Starting the computer...");
        cpu.Freeze();
        memory.Load(0, "BootLoader");
        cpu.Jump(0);
        cpu.Execute();
        Console.WriteLine("Computer started.");
    }
```

```
  public string ReadData()
  {
     return hardDrive.Read(100, 8);
  }
}
```

```
ComputerFacade computer = new ComputerFacade();
computer.Start();

string data = computer.ReadData();
Console.WriteLine($"Read data from hard drive: {data}");

/*Output:
Starting the computer...
CPU: Freezing...
Memory: Loading data 'BootLoader' to memory address 0
CPU: Jumping to memory address 0
CPU: Executing...
Computer started.
Hard Drive: Reading 8 bytes from LBA 100
Read data from hard drive: Data from Hard Drive */
```

Subsystems (CPU, Memory, and HardDrive) represent the complex components of a computer system.

The ComputerFacade acts as the Facade and provides simplified methods (Start and ReadData) for starting the computer and reading data from the hard drive.

The client, represented by the Program class, uses the ComputerFacade to perform computer-related tasks. The client does not need to interact directly with the subsystems or be aware of their complexities.

Behavioral Patterns

Behavioral design patterns focus on defining how objects interact and communicate with each other to accomplish specific tasks. These patterns provide solutions for the effective communication and collaboration of objects.

Observer Pattern

Defines a one-to-many dependency between objects so that when one object changes state, all its dependents are notified and updated automatically. Useful for implementing distributed event handling systems, where one object (the subject) needs to notify multiple observers about changes.

Key components of the Observer Pattern include:

Subject (or Observable): This is the object that is being observed. It maintains a collection of observers and notifies them when its state changes. The Subject provides methods for attaching, detaching, and notifying observers.

Observer: This is the interface or abstract class that defines the update method, which is called by the Subject when its state changes. Concrete Observer classes implement this interface.

Concrete Subject: This is a class that extends or implements the Subject interface and maintains the state that is being observed. It is responsible for notifying its observers when its state changes.

Concrete Observer: These are classes that implement the Observer interface and register with a Concrete Subject to receive notifications. When the state of the Concrete Subject changes, it calls the update method on all registered observers.

```csharp
// Observer interface
public interface IObserver
{
    void Update(string message);
}
// Concrete Observer
public class ConcreteObserver : IObserver
{
    private string name;

    public ConcreteObserver(string name)
    {
        this.name = name;
    }
    public void Update(string message)
    {
        Console.WriteLine($"{name} received message: {message}");
    }
}
```

```csharp
// Subject interface
public interface ISubject
{
    void RegisterObserver(IObserver observer);
    void RemoveObserver(IObserver observer);
    void NotifyObservers(string message);
}

// Concrete Subject
public class ConcreteSubject : ISubject
{
    private List<IObserver> observers = new List<IObserver>();

    public void RegisterObserver(IObserver observer)
    {
        observers.Add(observer);
    }

    public void RemoveObserver(IObserver observer)
    {
        observers.Remove(observer);
    }

    public void NotifyObservers(string message)
    {
        foreach (var observer in observers)
        {
            observer.Update(message);
        }
    }

    public void DoSomething()
    {
        Console.WriteLine("Subject is doing something.");
        NotifyObservers("State changed.");
    }
}
```

```csharp
ConcreteSubject subject = new ConcreteSubject();
IObserver observer1 = new ConcreteObserver("Observer 1");
IObserver observer2 = new ConcreteObserver("Observer 2");

subject.RegisterObserver(observer1);
subject.RegisterObserver(observer2);

subject.DoSomething();
```

The IObserver interface defines the Update method, which is called by the subject to notify observers of changes.

ConcreteObserver is a concrete implementation of the observer that receives and displays messages.

The ISubject interface defines methods for registering, removing, and notifying observers.

ConcreteSubject is a concrete implementation of the subject. When DoSomething is called, it notifies its registered observers.

We create a ConcreteSubject, register two observers, and then call DoSomething, which triggers the notification of observers.

Strategy Pattern

Defines a family of algorithms, encapsulates each one, and makes them interchangeable. Allows clients to choose the appropriate algorithm to use at runtime, providing flexibility and extensibility.

Key components of the Strategy Pattern include:

Context: This is the class that maintains a reference to the strategy object and can switch between different strategies. The context delegates the work to the strategy object and does not contain the implementation details of the algorithms.

Strategy: This is the interface or abstract class that defines a family of algorithms. Concrete strategies implement this interface and provide specific implementations of the algorithm

```csharp
// Strategy interface
public interface IStrategy
{
    void Execute();
}

// Concrete Strategies
public class ConcreteStrategyA : IStrategy
{
    public void Execute()
    {
        Console.WriteLine("Executing strategy A");
    }
}

public class ConcreteStrategyB : IStrategy
{
    public void Execute()
    {
        Console.WriteLine("Executing strategy B");
    }
}

// Context
public class Context
{
    private IStrategy strategy;

    public Context(IStrategy strategy)
    {
        this.strategy = strategy;
    }

    public void SetStrategy(IStrategy strategy)
    {
        this.strategy = strategy;
    }

    public void ExecuteStrategy()
    {
        strategy.Execute();
    }
}
```

```
IStrategy strategyA = new ConcreteStrategyA();
IStrategy strategyB = new ConcreteStrategyB();

Context context = new Context(strategyA);

context.ExecuteStrategy(); // Output: Executing strategy A

context.SetStrategy(strategyB);
context.ExecuteStrategy(); // Output: Executing strategy B
```

The IStrategy interface defines the strategy's contract with a single Execute method that concrete strategies must implement.

ConcreteStrategyA and ConcreteStrategyB are two concrete strategies that implement the IStrategy interface and provide specific implementations.

The Context class maintains a reference to the current strategy and provides methods to change the strategy or execute the current one.

We create instances of concrete strategies and a context. We set the context's strategy to either strategyA or strategyB and execute the strategy accordingly.

Command Pattern

Encapsulates a request as an object, thereby allowing for parameterization of clients with queues, requests, and operations. Useful for implementing undo/redo functionality, remote controls, and queuing requests.

Key components of the Command Pattern include:

Command: This is an interface or abstract class that declares a method for executing an action. The Command typically holds references to objects (receivers) that will perform the requested action when the Execute method is called.

Concrete Command: These are concrete implementations of the Command interface. They specify which action should be executed. Each Concrete Command holds a reference to the receiver and invokes specific methods on the receiver.

Receiver: This is the class that contains the actual implementation of actions. The Receiver knows how to perform the requested operation.

Invoker: The Invoker is responsible for holding and executing commands. It doesn't know the specific details of how the command works but triggers it when needed.

```csharp
// Command interface
public interface ICommand
{
    void Execute();
}

// Receiver
public class Light
{
    public void TurnOn()
    {
        Console.WriteLine("Light is on");
    }

    public void TurnOff()
    {
        Console.WriteLine("Light is off");
    }
}

// Concrete Commands
public class TurnOnCommand : ICommand
{
    private Light light;

    public TurnOnCommand(Light light)
    {
        this.light = light;
    }

    public void Execute()
    {
        light.TurnOn();
    }
}

public class TurnOffCommand : ICommand
{
    private Light light;

    public TurnOffCommand(Light light)
    {
        this.light = light;
    }
}
```

```csharp
    public void Execute()
    {
      light.TurnOff();
    }
}

// Invoker
public class RemoteControl
{
    private List<ICommand> commands = new List<ICommand>();

    public void AddCommand(ICommand command)
    {
      commands.Add(command);
    }

    public void ExecuteCommands()
    {
      foreach (var command in commands)
      {
        command.Execute();
      }
    }
}
```

```csharp
Light light = new Light();
ICommand turnOn = new TurnOnCommand(light);
ICommand turnOff = new TurnOffCommand(light);

RemoteControl remote = new RemoteControl();
remote.AddCommand(turnOn);
remote.AddCommand(turnOff);

remote.ExecuteCommands();

/*Output:
Light is on
Light is off
*/
```

The ICommand interface defines the Execute method that concrete commands must implement.

TurnOnCommand and TurnOffCommand are concrete command classes that encapsulate specific actions to turn the light on and off. They hold references to the Light receiver.

85

The Light class is the receiver that knows how to perform the actions.

The RemoteControl is the invoker that holds a list of commands and can execute them.

We create a Light receiver, concrete commands, add them to a remote control, and execute the commands.

State Pattern

Allows an object to alter its behavior when its internal state changes. The object will appear to change its class. Useful for modeling objects with complex state machines, such as game characters or workflows.

Key components of the State Pattern include:

Context: This is the class that maintains an instance of the current state and is responsible for switching between different states. The context delegates state-specific behavior to the current state object.

State: This is the interface or abstract class that defines a set of methods that concrete states must implement. These methods represent state-specific behavior.

Concrete State: These are concrete implementations of the state interface. Each concrete state class represents a specific state of the context and provides the implementation for state-specific behavior.

```csharp
// State interface
public interface IState
{
    void Handle(Context context);
}

// Concrete States
public class StateA : IState
{
    public void Handle(Context context)
    {
        Console.WriteLine("State A handling the request.");
        context.State = new StateB(); // Transition to State B
    }
}

public class StateB : IState
{
    public void Handle(Context context)
    {
        Console.WriteLine("State B handling the request.");
        context.State = new StateA(); // Transition to State A
    }
}

// Context
public class Context
{
    private IState state;

    public Context()
    {
        state = new StateA(); // Initial state
    }

    public IState State
    {
        get { return state; }
        set { state = value; }
    }

    public void Request()
    {
        state.Handle(this); // Delegates the request to the
                            // current state
    }
}
```

```
Context context = new Context();

// Repeatedly make requests, which cause state transitions
// between State A and State B.
context.Request(); // State A handling the request.
context.Request(); // State B handling the request.
context.Request(); // State A handling the request.
```

The IState interface defines the Handle method, which concrete states must implement to provide state-specific behavior.

StateA and StateB are concrete state classes representing different states. They provide the implementation for handling requests and changing the state of the context.

The Context class maintains the current state and delegates requests to the current state. It provides a mechanism to transition between states.

We create a context with an initial state of StateA. Repeatedly making requests results in state transitions between StateA and StateB.

Chain of Responsibility Pattern

Passes the request along a chain of handlers. Upon receiving a request, each handler decides whether to process it or pass it to the next handler in the chain.

Useful for building systems where multiple objects can handle a request without the sender needing to know which object will ultimately process it.

Key components of the Chain of Responsibility Pattern include:

Handler: This is an interface or abstract class that defines a method for handling requests and contains a reference to the next handler in the chain. Handlers can process the request, delegate it to the next handler, or stop processing.

Concrete Handler: These are concrete implementations of the Handler interface. Each Concrete Handler decides whether to process the request, delegate it to the next handler, or terminate the chain.

Client: The client initiates the request and starts the chain. It's responsible for creating and configuring the chain, including adding handlers to the chain.

```csharp
// Handler interface
public abstract class Handler
{
    protected Handler successor;

    public void SetSuccessor(Handler successor)
    {
        this.successor = successor;
    }

    public abstract void HandleRequest(int request);
}

// Concrete Handlers
public class ConcreteHandler1 : Handler
{
    public override void HandleRequest(int request)
    {
        if (request < 10)
        {
            Console.WriteLine("ConcreteHandler1 is handling the
                                request.");
        }
        else if (successor != null)
        {
            successor.HandleRequest(request);
        }
    }
}

public class ConcreteHandler2 : Handler
{
    public override void HandleRequest(int request)
    {
        if (request >= 10 && request < 20)
        {
            Console.WriteLine("ConcreteHandler2 is handling the
                                request.");
        }
        else if (successor != null)
        {
            successor.HandleRequest(request);
        }
    }
}
```

```csharp
public class ConcreteHandler3 : Handler
{
    public override void HandleRequest(int request)
    {
        if (request >= 20)
        {
            Console.WriteLine("ConcreteHandler3 is handling the
                                    request.");
        }
        else
        {
            Console.WriteLine("Request cannot be handled.");
        }
    }
}
```

```csharp
Handler handler1 = new ConcreteHandler1();
Handler handler2 = new ConcreteHandler2();
Handler handler3 = new ConcreteHandler3();

handler1.SetSuccessor(handler2);
handler2.SetSuccessor(handler3);

// Start the request with handler1
handler1.HandleRequest(5);//Output: ConcreteHandler1 is handling the request.
handler1.HandleRequest(15);//Output: ConcreteHandler2 is handling the request.
handler1.HandleRequest(25);//Output: ConcreteHandler3 is handling the request.
handler1.HandleRequest(8);// Output: ConcreteHandler1 is handling the request.
```

The Handler abstract class defines a HandleRequest method, which concrete handlers must implement. It also contains a reference to the next handler in the chain.

ConcreteHandler1, ConcreteHandler2, and ConcreteHandler3 are concrete handler classes that process requests based on specific criteria. They may delegate to the next handler in the chain if necessary.

We configures the chain of handlers and initiates requests through handler1.

90

Template Method Pattern

Defines the program skeleton in a method, deferring some steps to subclasses.

Useful when you want to let subclasses redefine specific steps of an algorithm without changing its overall structure.

Key components of the Template Method Pattern include:

Abstract Class: This is the base class that defines the template method, which consists of a series of steps. Some of these steps are implemented in the base class, while others are declared as abstract methods that must be implemented by concrete subclasses.

Concrete Classes: These are the subclasses that inherit from the abstract base class and provide concrete implementations for the abstract methods. These implementations customize the algorithm defined in the template method.

```csharp
// Abstract class (AbstractTemplate) with the template method
public abstract class AbstractTemplate
{
    public void TemplateMethod()
    {
        Step1();
        Step2();
        Step3();
    }

    protected abstract void Step1();
    protected abstract void Step2();

    protected void Step3()
    {
        Console.WriteLine("AbstractTemplate: Default
                        implementation of Step3");
    }
}

// Concrete subclass (ConcreteTemplate) that extends the abstract// class
```

```
public class ConcreteTemplate : AbstractTemplate
{
    protected override void Step1()
    {
        Console.WriteLine("ConcreteTemplate: Step1 implementation");
    }

    protected override void Step2()
    {
        Console.WriteLine("ConcreteTemplate: Step2 implementation");
    }
}
```

```
AbstractTemplate template = new ConcreteTemplate();
template.TemplateMethod();

/*Output:
ConcreteTemplate: Step1 implementation
ConcreteTemplate: Step2 implementation
AbstractTemplate: Default implementation of Step3
*/
```

The AbstractTemplate class defines the template method TemplateMethod that consists of three steps: Step1, Step2, and Step3. Step3 has a default implementation in the abstract class.

The ConcreteTemplate class extends AbstractTemplate and provides concrete implementations for Step1 and Step2. It leaves Step3 with the default implementation.

We create an instance of ConcreteTemplate and call its TemplateMethod. The template method is executed, and each step is invoked, including the default implementation of Step3 in the base class.

Visitor Pattern

Represents an operation to be performed on the elements of an object structure.

Allows you to add new operations to existing object structures without modifying them.

Key components of the Visitor Pattern include:

Visitor Interface: This interface declares a set of visit methods, each of which corresponds to a specific type of element in the object structure. Each visit method takes an element as an argument.

Concrete Visitor: These are concrete implementations of the visitor interface. Each concrete visitor provides specific behavior for each type of element in the object structure.

Element Interface: This interface declares an Accept method, which accepts a visitor as an argument. The Accept method allows the visitor to visit the element and perform its operations.

Concrete Element: These are concrete implementations of the element interface. Each concrete element implements the Accept method and typically stores some data that the visitor can operate on.

Object Structure: This is a collection or hierarchy of objects (elements) that can be visited by the visitor. It typically provides a method to iterate through its elements and call the Accept method of each element.

```
// Visitor interface
public interface IVisitor
{
    void Visit(ConcreteElementA elementA);
    void Visit(ConcreteElementB elementB);
}
// Concrete Visitor
public class ConcreteVisitor : IVisitor
{
    public void Visit(ConcreteElementA elementA)
    {
     Console.WriteLine("Visitor is processing ConcreteElementA");
    }
    public void Visit(ConcreteElementB elementB)
    {
     Console.WriteLine("Visitor is processing ConcreteElementB");
```

```csharp
      }
}

// Element interface
public interface IElement
{
   void Accept(IVisitor visitor);
}

// Concrete Elements
public class ConcreteElementA : IElement
{
   public void Accept(IVisitor visitor)
   {
      visitor.Visit(this);
   }

   public void OperationA()
   {
      Console.WriteLine("Operation A of ConcreteElementA");
   }
}

public class ConcreteElementB : IElement
{
   public void Accept(IVisitor visitor)
   {
      visitor.Visit(this);
   }

   public void OperationB()
   {
      Console.WriteLine("Operation B of ConcreteElementB");
   }
}
// Object Structure
public class ObjectStructure
{
   private IElement[] elements;

   public ObjectStructure()
   {
      elements = new IElement[] { new ConcreteElementA(),
                        new ConcreteElementB() };
   }

   public void Accept(IVisitor visitor)
   {
      foreach (var element in elements)
```

```
        {
            element.Accept(visitor);
        }
    }
}
```

The IVisitor interface declares two visit methods corresponding to two concrete element types.

ConcreteVisitor is a concrete visitor that implements the visit methods to provide specific behavior for each concrete element type.

The IElement interface declares an Accept method that accepts a visitor.

ConcreteElementA and ConcreteElementB are concrete elements that implement the Accept method and can execute specific operations.

The ObjectStructure is a collection of elements and provides a method to accept a visitor and iterate through its elements, invoking the Accept method of each element.

We create a visitor, an object structure with elements, and call the Accept method to allow the visitor to visit each element.

Interpreter Pattern

Provides a way to evaluate language grammar or expressions. Useful for implementing interpreters for domain-specific languages.

Key components of the Interpreter Pattern include:

Abstract Expression: This is the abstract class or interface that represents expressions in the language. It declares an Interpret method that concrete expressions must implement. The Interpret method is responsible for evaluating the expression.

Terminal Expression: These are concrete expression classes that represent the terminal symbols in the language. Terminal expressions perform simple evaluations and have no sub-expressions.

Non-terminal Expression: These are concrete expression classes that represent non-terminal symbols in the language. Non-terminal expressions can contain other expressions, forming complex expressions. They implement the Interpret method by interpreting their sub-expressions.

Context: The context contains information that is global to the interpreter and is used by expressions during interpretation.

Client: The client is responsible for creating the abstract syntax tree (AST) of expressions and invoking the Interpret method to evaluate or process sentences.

```
// Abstract Expression
public abstract class Expression
{
    public abstract int Interpret();
}

// Terminal Expressions
public class NumberExpression : Expression
{
    private int number;

    public NumberExpression(int number)
    {
        this.number = number;
    }
}
```

```csharp
  public override int Interpret()
  {
    return number;
  }
}

// Non-terminal Expressions
public class AdditionExpression : Expression
{
  private Expression left;
  private Expression right;

  public AdditionExpression(Expression left, Expression right)
  {
    this.left = left;
    this.right = right;
  }

  public override int Interpret()
  {
    return left.Interpret() + right.Interpret();
  }
}

public class SubtractionExpression : Expression
{
  private Expression left;
  private Expression right;

  public SubtractionExpression(Expression left,
                               Expression right)
  {
    this.left = left;
    this.right = right;
  }

  public override int Interpret()
  {
    return left.Interpret() - right.Interpret();
  }
}
```

```
Expression expression = new AdditionExpression(
    new NumberExpression(5),
    new SubtractionExpression(
        new NumberExpression(10),
        new NumberExpression(2)
    )
);

int result = expression.Interpret();
Console.WriteLine("Result: " + result); // Output: Result: 13
```

Expression is the abstract expression class that declares the Interpret method.

NumberExpression is a terminal expression representing a number.

AdditionExpression and SubtractionExpression are non-terminal expressions that interpret addition and subtraction, respectively, by evaluating their sub-expressions.

We create an abstract syntax tree (AST) for a simple arithmetic expression and evaluate it by invoking the Interpret method on the root expression.

Mediator Pattern

Defines an object that encapsulates how a set of objects interact. It promotes loose coupling by keeping objects from referring to each other explicitly. Useful when communication between objects becomes complex and leads to tight coupling.

Key components of the Mediator Pattern include:

Mediator: This is an interface or an abstract class that defines the communication protocol between objects. It typically contains methods for registering, notifying, and managing colleagues (objects that communicate through the mediator).

Concrete Mediator: This is a concrete implementation of the mediator interface. It knows about and manages colleagues, ensuring that they communicate effectively by routing messages and maintaining references to them.

Colleague: Colleagues are objects that need to communicate with each other but do so through the mediator. Colleagues typically do not have direct references to each other and only know about the mediator. They use the mediator to send and receive messages.

```csharp
// Mediator interface
public interface IMediator
{
    void Register(Colleague colleague);
    void Send(string message, Colleague colleague);
}

// Concrete Mediator
public class ConcreteMediator : IMediator
{
    private List<Colleague> colleagues = new List<Colleague>();

    public void Register(Colleague colleague)
    {
        colleagues.Add(colleague);
    }

    public void Send(string message, Colleague sender)
    {
        foreach (var colleague in colleagues)
        {
            if (colleague != sender)
            {
                colleague.Receive(message);
            }
        }
    }
}

// Colleague
public abstract class Colleague
{
    protected IMediator mediator;

    public Colleague(IMediator mediator)
    {
        this.mediator = mediator;
    }

    public abstract void Send(string message);
    public abstract void Receive(string message);
}

// Concrete Colleague
public class ConcreteColleagueA : Colleague
{
```

```csharp
    public ConcreteColleagueA(IMediator mediator) :
                        base(mediator) { }

    public override void Send(string message)
    {
        Console.WriteLine($"Colleague A sends a message:
                            {message}");
        mediator.Send(message, this);
    }

    public override void Receive(string message)
    {
        Console.WriteLine($"Colleague A receives a message:
                            {message}");
    }
}
public class ConcreteColleagueB : Colleague
{
    public ConcreteColleagueB(IMediator mediator) :
                        base(mediator) { }

    public override void Send(string message)
    {
        Console.WriteLine($"Colleague B sends a message:
                            {message}");
        mediator.Send(message, this);
    }

    public override void Receive(string message)
    {
        Console.WriteLine($"Colleague B receives a message:
                            {message}");
    }
}
```

```csharp
IMediator mediator = new ConcreteMediator();
Colleague colleagueA = new ConcreteColleagueA(mediator);
Colleague colleagueB = new ConcreteColleagueB(mediator);

mediator.Register(colleagueA);
mediator.Register(colleagueB);
colleagueA.Send("Hello from Colleague A");
colleagueB.Send("Hi from Colleague B");
/*Output:
Colleague A sends a message: Hello from Colleague A
Colleague B receives a message: Hello from Colleague A
Colleague B sends a message: Hi from Colleague B
```

IMediator is the mediator interface with methods for registering colleagues and sending messages.

ConcreteMediator is a concrete mediator that maintains a list of registered colleagues and routes messages between them.

Colleague is an abstract class that represents colleagues. Colleagues have a reference to the mediator and abstract methods for sending and receiving messages.

ConcreteColleagueA and ConcreteColleagueB are concrete colleagues that implement the send and receive methods. They use the mediator to send and receive messages.

We create a mediator, colleagues, and register them with the mediator. Colleagues send and receive messages through the mediator.

Memento Pattern

Captures and externalizes an object's internal state so the object can be restored to this state later. Useful for implementing undo mechanisms and restoring an object's state.

Key components of the Memento Pattern include:

Originator: This is the object for which you want to capture and restore the state. The originator has two main responsibilities: saving its current state (creating a memento) and restoring its state from a memento.

Memento: The memento is an object that stores the state of the originator. It may include one or more properties to capture the state of the originator.

Caretaker: The caretaker is responsible for keeping track of mementos. It holds references to multiple mementos and can request the originator to save or restore its state from a memento.

101

```csharp
// Memento (stores the state)
public class Memento
{
    public string State { get; }

    public Memento(string state)
    {
        State = state;
    }
}

// Originator (object to capture and restore state)
public class Originator
{
    private string state;

    public string State
    {
        get => state;
        set
        {
            state = value;
            Console.WriteLine($"Originator's state has changed
                                to: {state}");
        }
    }

    public Memento CreateMemento()
    {
        return new Memento(state);
    }

    public void RestoreFromMemento(Memento memento)
    {
        state = memento.State;
        Console.WriteLine($"Originator's state has been restored
                                to: {state}");
    }
}

// Caretaker (manages mementos)
public class Caretaker
{
    public Memento Memento { get; set; }
}
```

```
Originator originator = new Originator();
Caretaker caretaker = new Caretaker();

// Set and save the state
originator.State = "State 1";
caretaker.Memento = originator.CreateMemento();

// Change the state
originator.State = "State 2";

// Restore the state from the saved memento
originator.RestoreFromMemento(caretaker.Memento);

/*Output:
 Originator's state has changed to: State 1
 Originator's state has changed to: State 2
 Originator's state has been restored to: State 1
*/
```

The Memento class stores the state of the Originator.

The Originator class has a State property, which is the state to be captured and restored. It provides methods to create a memento of its state and restore its state from a memento.

The Caretaker class holds a reference to a memento. It's responsible for managing and keeping track of mementos.

We create an Originator and a Caretaker. We set the state, save a memento, change the state, and then restore the state from the saved memento.

Architectural patterns

Architectural patterns are high-level structural patterns that provide guidelines and best practices for organizing the overall structure of software systems. They define the relationships and interactions between major components of a software application, helping to ensure that the application is scalable, maintainable, and follows good design principles.

Model-View-Controller (MVC) Pattern

Separates the application into three interconnected components: Model (data and business logic), View (presentation and user interface), and Controller (manages user input and interaction). Promotes a clear separation of concerns, making it easier to maintain and extend the application.

View: Depending on the technology you use to develop the app, it can be a CSHTML page or ASPX page among other options.

Model: A class that contains the data of the request or returns data for the response.

Controller: Functions that take the models, transfer the data to the view, and return the view populated with data from the model.

Example with ASP.NET MVC:

Model

```csharp
public class LoginModel
{
    public string Email;
    public string Password;

    public bool IsValid()
    {
        // check database if Email and Password are valid
        return true;
    }
}
```

The LoginModel class represents the data associated with the login operation. It has two public fields, "Email" and "Password," which are used to store the user's login credentials.

The IsValid method is a placeholder that is meant to check the user's credentials against a database (or some form of authentication) to determine if the login is valid. In the current example, it always returns true, so the login is considered valid.

Controller

```
public class HomeController : Controller
{
    [HttpGet("login")]
    public IActionResult Login()
    {
        return View("Login.cshtml", new LoginModel());
    }

    [HttpPost("login")]
    public IActionResult Login(LoginModel loginModel)
    {
        if (loginModel.IsValid())
        {
            return View("HomePage.cshtml");
        }
        else
        {
            return View("Error.cshtml");
        }
    }
}
```

HttpGet "login" Action: When a user accesses the "login" URL with a GET request, the Login action is invoked.

It returns the "Login.cshtml" view, rendering a login form, and passes an instance of the LoginModel to the view.

HttpPost "login" Action: When a user submits the login form via a POST request, the Login action with a LoginModel parameter is invoked.

It first checks if the submitted LoginModel is valid using the IsValid method.

If the LoginModel is considered valid, it redirects to the "HomePage.cshtml" view.

If the LoginModel is not valid, it redirects to the "Error.cshtml" view.

View

```
@model LoginModel

<form method="post" asp-action="Login">
 <div>
    <label>Email</label>
    <input asp-for="Email" type="text" />
 </div>
 <div>
    <label>Password</label>
    <input asp-for="Password" type="password" />
 </div>
 <button type="submit">Login</button>
</form>
```

It's strongly typed to the LoginModel, which is passed from the Login action as the model for this view.

It uses Razor syntax (@model, @{}, @if, asp-for) to define the structure and logic of the view.

It includes a form for user input (email and password) with labels and input fields. The asp-for attributes are used to bind the input fields to the properties of the LoginModel.

The login button submits the form to the "Login" action with a POST request.

MVVM - Model-View-ViewModel Pattern

Similar to MVC but tailored for UI development.

Separates the View logic from the View and introduces a ViewModel to manage the presentation logic.

Commonly used in client applications with complex user interfaces.

MVVM is commonly used in WPF app development. In MVVM, we pass the model data into a ViewModel object that refines the data, preparing it for binding to specific WPF components. This approach contributes to a cleaner and more structured view.

3-Tier Architecture

Divides the application into multiple logical layers (e.g., presentation, business, data access) with well-defined responsibilities and dependencies.

Enhances modularity and maintainability by enforcing a clear separation of concerns.

Common Naming for the layers:

Presentation: UI, PL

Business: BL, Services, Logic

DataAccess: DAL, Repository, DataBase, Data

The layer demonstrated in the MVC example is the presentation layer. Let's add the two additional layers.

```
public class LoginModel
{
    public string Email;
    public string Password;

    public bool IsValid()
    {
        return new BusinessLogic().IsValid(Email, Password);
    }
}

//business layer
public class BusinessLogic
{
    public bool IsValid(string email, string password)
    {
        //test if email validation logic
        return new DataAccess().IsEmailFound(email, password);
    }
}
//data access layer
public class DataAccess
{
    public bool IsEmailFound(string email, string password)
    {
        //test if email and password exist in db
        return true;
    }
}
```

BusinessLogic: Contains the business rules and logic for the login operation. It checks if the provided email is valid, and if so, it delegates to the Data Access layer to determine if the email and password exist in the database. In this example, it uses a simple IsEmailFound method to check for email and password existence.

DataAccess: Represents the layer responsible for interacting with a data source, typically a database. Contains a IsEmailFound method that simulates checking if an email and password exist in the database.

Microservices Architecture

Organizes the application as a collection of small, independent services that communicate with each other over a network. Supports scalability, flexibility, and ease of development and deployment but requires careful management of microservices.

Basically, instead of creating one large project, we break it down into smaller projects, each dedicated to a specific part of the overall project that can function independently as its own separate project.

Example: System that charge credit cards of different billings

Without Microservices Architecture: In this scenario, I would create a single service with classes for each type of billing, such as "VISABilling.cs" and "MasterCardBilling.cs."

With Microservices Architecture: In contrast, under the microservices architecture, I create a separate service for each type of billing. Initially, this may seem like an overhead, but it offers significant advantages. For instance, when a bug arises in a specific billing service, you only need to deploy updates for that particular service, minimizing the risk of downtime for the entire system. Additionally, if one billing service needs to adopt a new technology or undergo updates, you can make changes to that specific service without affecting all other services, reducing the risk of system-wide issues.

Repository Pattern

Separates the logic that retrieves data from data storage from the rest of the application. Provides a clean and consistent API for accessing data.

In the context of a 3-tier architecture example, we enhance the design by introducing a dedicated API project. Within this revised structure, we migrate the DataAccess layer into the API project and expose methods via API endpoints, consolidating the architectural layers from 3 to 2. With this adaptation, a new 'Client' component comes into play. The Business Logic layer now utilizes this client to interact with the API, offering improved separation of concerns, modularity, and scalability within the application's architecture.

www.ingramcontent.com/pod-product-compliance
Lightning Source LLC
Chambersburg PA
CBHW082216290526
45794CB00009B/3563